THE CURIOSITY BOX

ROCKS & FOSSILS

by Peter Riley

Illustrated by Krina Patel

W
FRANKLIN WATTS
LONDON·SYDNEY

Franklin Watts
First published in Great Britain in 2016 by The Watts Publishing Group

Text copyright © Peter Riley 2016

Credits
Series Editor: Amy Stephenson
Series Designer: Krina Patel
Illustrations: Krina Patel
Picture Researcher: Amy Stephenson / Diana Morris

ISBN: 978 1 4451 4640 9

Printed in China

MIX
Paper from
responsible sources
FSC® C104740
www.fsc.org

Franklin Watts
An imprint of
Hachette Children's Group
Part of The Watts Publishing Group
Carmelite House
50 Victoria Embankment
London EC4Y 0DZ

An Hachette UK Company
www.hachette.co.uk

www.franklinwatts.co.uk

To Michael and Rita — PR

To Rekha and Yashwant Patel — KP

CONTENTS

⚠ This symbol shows where there is some information to help you stay safe.
Words in **bold** can be found in the glossary on page 30.

WHAT ARE ROCKS AND FOSSILS?

Have you got a special pebble? A pebble is a small rock. Perhaps you have seen some fossils in a museum. You can find out many curious things about rocks and fossils in this book.

Sometimes you have to guess what you see, then turn the page to find the answer.

Many pebbles are smooth and rounded because water in rivers or the sea rubs them together.

Near the end of this book is our rocks and fossils curiosity box. You can talk about it with your friends.

You can make your own curiosity box of rocks and fossils if you visit a garden, a park, the seaside or the countryside.

ROCKS

Rocks are hard materials. They are formed from different types of **crystals** (*kris-tals*) called **minerals**. The crystals lock together to make the rock. For example, feldspar, mica and quartz crystals lock together to make granite rock.

feldspar + mica + quartz = granite

Some crystals can be easily seen, but most are so small you need a magnifying glass or **microscope** to see them.

Salt crystals under a microscope

FOSSILS

fish fossil

Fossils are the remains of plants and animals that lived long ago. If you look carefully at some rocks, you may see fossils that have formed in them.

Dinosaurs are animals that lived over 65 million years ago, but there aren't any alive today. We know about dinosaurs from their fossils, which have been found in rocks by scientists.

dinosaur fossil

EARTH – A ROCKY PLANET

If you look at soil with a magnifying glass, you may see tiny pieces of different kinds of rock in it.

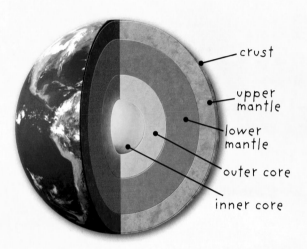

crust
upper mantle
lower mantle
outer core
inner core

If people dig deep enough into the soil they will reach solid rock. This is called BEDROCK.

Bedrock forms the top part of the Earth's CRUST. This is a thick layer of rock that goes all around the world, under the soil and the oceans.

Below the crust is another rocky layer called the MANTLE. It is very hot and can be up to 400 times hotter than boiling water — that's 4,000° Celsius! The mantle rock flows around slowly, like treacle.

At the centre of the Earth is the CORE. It is hotter than the mantle and has a temperature of 5,000° Celsius.

iron

nickel

The core is made from two metals — iron and nickel.

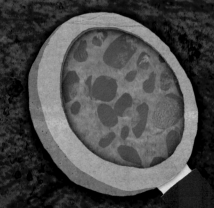

The crust is broken into huge pieces of rock called PLATES. The mantle rocks flowing below the plates move them about. All the land on Earth rests on the plates. The plates fit together like a jigsaw.

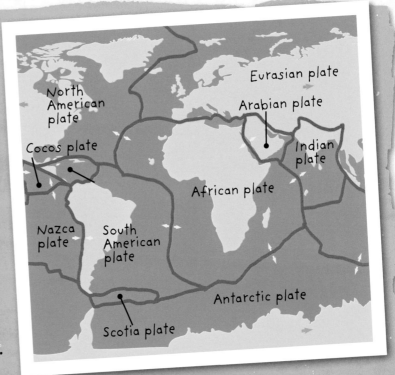

North American plate

Eurasian plate

Arabian plate

Cocos plate

Indian plate

African plate

Nazca plate

South American plate

Antarctic plate

Scotia plate

The plates move slowly. Some plates move only three millimetres in a month. That is as fast as your fingernails grow.

3mm

0   10mm

WHAT CAN THIS BE?

A pyramid?
A giant fossil?
A volcano?
Turn the page to find out.

VOLCANIC ROCKS

It's a volcano!

Volcanoes are found all over Earth where two plates push together. Under a volcano is hot rock called **MAGMA**.

Sometimes magma bursts out of the top of a volcano. This is called an ERUPTION.

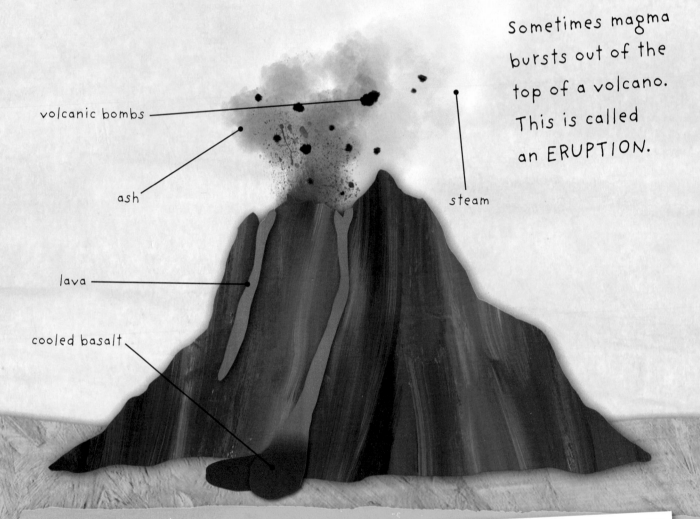

volcanic bombs

ash

steam

lava

cooled basalt

When a volcano erupts, it sends out clouds of steam. Ash and rocks called volcanic bombs, shoot up into the air.

Hot, liquid rock called LAVA flows down the sides of the volcano. It can take months for the lava to cool.

When lava cools it forms solid rock, such as these basalt columns.

There are other rocks that can form when a volcano erupts.

OBSIDIAN (ob-sid-ee-an) is a smooth rock made of black glass.

PUMICE (pum-iss) is rough and full of holes. It is the only rock that can float in water. Some people scrub this rock on their feet to remove dead skin!

PHONOLITE (fo-no-lite) is called 'clinker stone', because it makes a ringing sound when it is hit with a hammer.

WHAT CAN THIS BE?

Another volcano?
A giant rock formed in the Earth's crust?
A giant rock from outer space?
Turn the page to find out.

ROCKS IN THE CRUST

It's a giant rock formed in the Earth's crust!

Sometimes a huge amount of magma pushes up into the crust. If it doesn't erupt out of a volcano, it can cool down to form a rock called GRANITE. If a piece of granite is very large it is called a monolith (mon-o-lith).

This granite monolith is in California, USA. Why do you think it is named 'Half Dome'?

Like all rocks, granite is made from minerals. They join together in different ways to make different coloured granites (see page 5).

Granite is a very tough rock. It can be cut and polished and used for building.

raw granite

cut and polished

Earth's crust has many different kinds of rock in it, such as limestone, mudstone, granite and sandstone. When magma comes up into the crust, its heat bakes rocks that are close by.

When LIMESTONE is baked it turns into MARBLE. We use marble to make statues.

marble rock in the ground

marble rock in a statue

When MUDSTONE is baked it turns into SLATE. People break up slate into thin sheets and use it to cover roofs to keep out rain.

When GRANITE and SANDSTONE are baked, they turn into a stripy rock called GNEISS (*nice*). The stripes are layers of different minerals that line up as the rock bakes.

BREAKING UP

Rocks outside the crust slowly break up. Wind, rain, heat and cold can all make rocks change. We call this **WEATHERING**. Broken up rocks of different sizes are given different names.

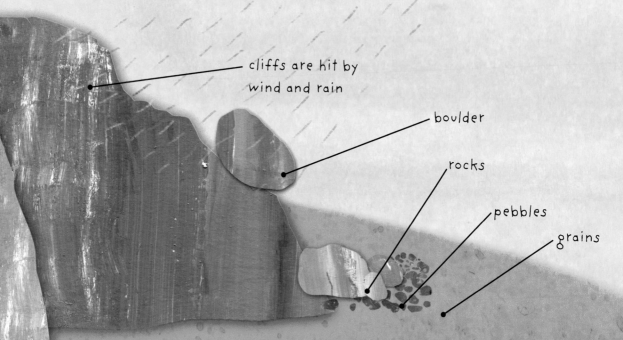

cliffs are hit by wind and rain

boulder

rocks

pebbles

grains

The seaside is a good place to see all of these sizes of rock.

There are different sizes of GRAINS. The largest grains are sand grains. Most sand is made of quartz. White sand is sometimes made of limestone.

SILT is a smaller grain than sand. CLAY is the smallest of the rocky grains.

yellow sand

white sand

silt

clay

Pebbles and grains can be broken down and moved by water. Grains can also be blown away by the wind. This movement of pebbles and grains is called **EROSION**.

When wind, streams, rivers, and waves in the sea move lots of pebbles or grains to another place, they can form new rocks. Over time, the weight of them crushes them together into rock.

Pebbles crushed together form rocks called conglomerates (con-glom-er-ates).

Sand grains make rocks called sandstone.

Silt and clay make mudstone rocks, such as siltstone.

Clay makes a rock called claystone.

WHAT CAN THIS BE?

A rock painted white?
A rock made from white sand?
A rock made from tiny shells?
Turn the page to find out.

ROCKS MADE FROM OTHER THINGS

It's a rock made from tiny shells!

The SHELL is called a coccolith (ko-ko-lith). You need a microscope to see each shell.

Coccolith shells are made by **algae** (al-gee) that live in the sea. When the algae die, the shells sink to the sea floor, stick together and form a rock called CHALK.

The shells of sea animals, such as **scallops,** can also make rock. When these animals die, their shells also sink to the sea floor, stick together and form a rock called LIMESTONE.

14

Some MAN-MADE materials are as hard as rock. Sometimes pieces of them can look like **natural** rocks. Brick, **cement** and **concrete** are used to make buildings. They are made from lots of different types of natural rock that are crushed and mixed with water. The water helps the rocks stick together. Bricks are often baked to make them hard, and concrete hardens when it dries.

broken bricks look like red rocks

broken cement looks like grey rocks

broken concrete looks like speckled rocks

Clay is a natural rock that can be shaped and baked to make man-made things, such as pots and tiles.

CAVES AND MINES

There are natural and man-made holes in the Earth's crust. A cave is a natural hole inside rocky ground. A man-made hole is called a mine. People sometimes go into these holes.

A cave's entrance is called the 'mouth'. Inside the cave there may be long, narrow tunnels and large open spaces called caverns. You may be lucky enough to visit a cave or a mine.
⚠️ Never enter a cave or mine on your own. You must always have an adult with you.

Rainwater helps to form some caves in limestone rock.
It **dissolves** the rock as it moves through it.
A cave forms where the rock has been dissolved.

After a cave has formed, water can still drip into it. Each drop leaves a little piece of **calcite** on the cave ceiling as it falls from it. In time, these pieces form **stalactites**.

When a drop splashes onto the cave floor, it leaves another piece of calcite behind. In time these pieces form **stalagmites**.

Sometimes stalagmites and stalactites join together and form a column of rock.

These white veins are made from the mineral, quartz.

Sometimes hot magma rises up through cracks in the Earth's crust and then cools down. It can form *VEINS* inside the cracks.

Some veins have useful materials in them. A *MINE* is dug to get them out. Some kinds of magma form veins with metals in them. Other veins have coal (see page 20) in them.

In mines, veins are broken up with tools and machines. The useful materials are collected from the broken-up rocks.

This machine is working in a coal mine. Dead plants can form veins of coal.

WHAT CAN THIS BE?

A metal?
A gemstone?
A yellow stone?
Turn the page to find out.

It's a metal!

This metal is called gold. People have used gold to make jewellery for thousands of years.

Gold is softer than most other metals and can easily be shaped.

Silver and copper are two other metals that can be found in veins.

Other metals, such as iron, zinc and tin, form minerals called ORES. These ores look like rocks and have rocky material in them.

silver nugget

silver lamp

copper nugget

copper wire

tin ore – stannite

iron ore – hematite

Furnaces have to be very hot to make the metal flow out of the rocky ores.

When ore is heated in a **furnace**, the metal melts and flows out of the rocky material. The liquid metal is collected and cooled.

When it is cold, the metal forms a solid block. The block can be melted again to make useful metal items, such as nails and cans.

GEMSTONES can also form in veins when magma cools down. Gems form crystals that may be clear or cloudy, colourful or colourless.

Some gemstones sparkle when light shines on them.

emerald gemstone in rock

People carefully take gems out of the rocks. They cut and polish them and make them into jewellery.

diamond

colourless and clear

emerald

colourful and clear

jasper

colourful and cloudy

opal

colourful and cloudy

ruby

colourful and clear

sapphire

colourful and clear

19

COAL AND SANDSTONE FOSSILS

Millions of years ago there were huge **swamps** on Earth. When swamp plants died and fell into the swamp, some did not **rot**.

The plants piled up on top of each other. As they got squashed together, they broke down to make a black rock called COAL.

Some plants that fell into the swamp turned
into rock but kept their plant shapes.
They became FOSSIL PLANTS.
Many fossil plants look like the ferns and
horsetails that still grow on Earth today.

fossil fern

living fern

fossil horsetail

living horsetail

You can find fossil plants and animals in rocks that form from tiny pieces, such as SANDSTONE. It can take thousands of years for fossils to form.

1. If a dead animal is covered with sand, its body will not rot.

2. The sand around the dead animal slowly gets thicker, squashes together and turns to sandstone rock. The soft parts of the animal break up, but the hard bones remain.

sand

sandstone

3. Water moves through the sand and rock. It contains minerals. As the water flows in and around the bones, the minerals take the place of the bones and become fossils.

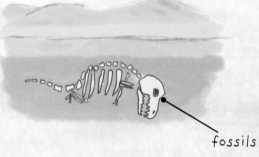

fossils

WHAT CAN THIS BE?

A fossil of an **ancient** sea animal?
A fossil of an ancient land animal?
A fossil of an ancient plant?
Turn the page to find out.

It's a fossil of an ancient sea animal!

The animal is an invertebrate (*in-ver-teh-brate*) called a **trilobite** (*tril-oh-bite*).

Invertebrates are animals that do not have bones in their bodies. Many have hard shells instead. Their shells can turn into fossils.

trilobite

ammonite

belemnite

Animals called **ammonites** (*am-on-ites*) and **belemnites** (*be-lem-nites*) also swam in the ancient seas.

Ammonites had coiled shells and belemnites had straight, pointed shells.

ammonite fossils

belemnite fossil

Here are some common invertebrate fossils.

devil's claw

coral

snail

mussel

starfish

brachiopod
(bra-kee-oh-pod)

crinoid

WHAT CAN THIS BE?

A tooth fossil?
A scale fossil?
A claw fossil?
Turn the page to find out.

MORE ANIMAL FOSSILS!

It's a tooth fossil from a fish called a shark!

VERTEBRATES (ver-teh-brates) are animals with a skeleton that is usually made of bone. Their bones can form fossils.

Most fish have skeletons made of bone.

fossil fish

SHARKS are fish that have skeletons made of **cartilage** (car-tih-lage). Cartilage rots away and is not hard enough to form fossils.

A shark's TEETH are made of much harder material than cartilage, so they can form fossils.

Sharks have lots of very sharp teeth!

Fossils of many types of vertebrates have been found. People have found fossils of **amphibians**, **mammals**, birds and **reptiles**.

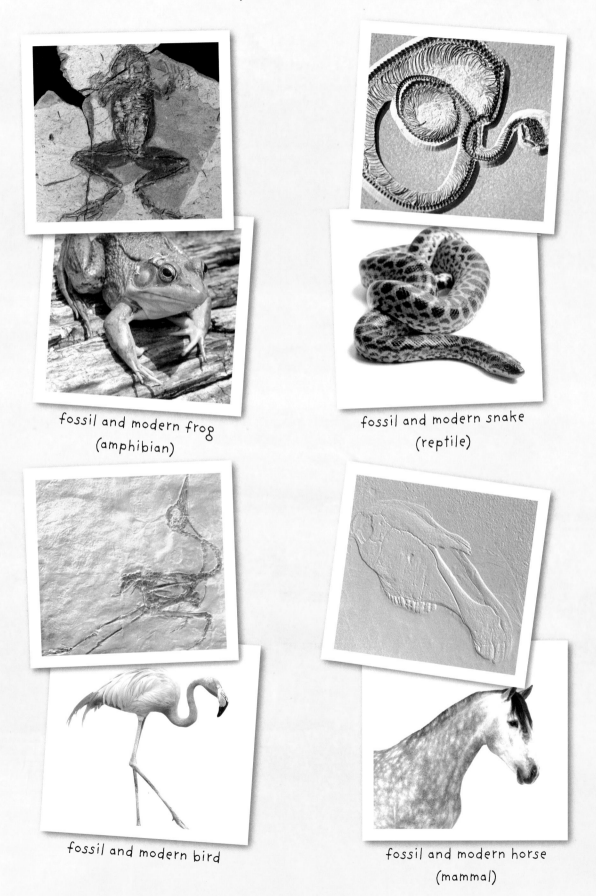

fossil and modern frog
(amphibian)

fossil and modern snake
(reptile)

fossil and modern bird

fossil and modern horse
(mammal)

TRACE FOSSILS

Sometimes living things leave TRACE FOSSILS. These are not fossils of dead animals or plants, they are fossils of things made by an animal's body, when it was alive.

Worms that lived long ago made BURROWS, which turned into fossils.

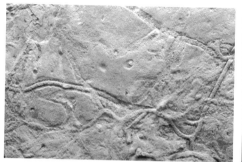

The wavy lines on this rock were once worm burrows.

Footprints are the most famous trace fossils. When footprints are in a line, they are called a TRACKWAY. This is a trackway in Arizona, USA. It was made by a dinosaur that lived over 190 million years ago!

Millions of years ago a dinosaur walked here.

This trace fossil shows the dinosaur had three toes.

DINOSAURS have left a large number of trace fossils, which have helped us learn about these **extinct** animals. They left trackways and fossil eggs.

These dinosaur eggs didn't **hatch**. Over time the eggshell became a trace fossil.

Some dinosaurs have even left fossil poo!

poo

trackway

ROCKS AND FOSSILS CURIOSITY BOX

A curiosity box is a place to put all of the curious things you have collected.

What items are in your rocks and fossils curiosity box?

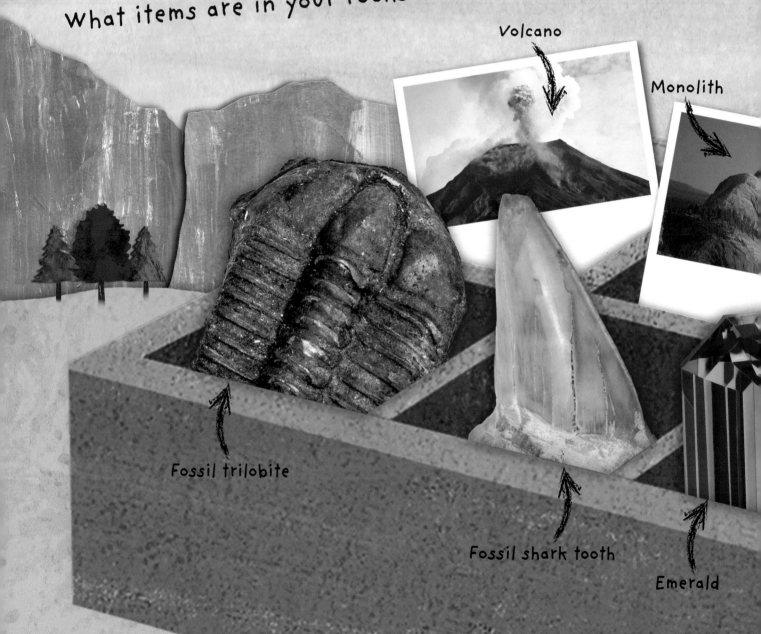

Volcano

Monolith

Fossil trilobite

Fossil shark tooth

Emerald

CURIOUS QUIZ

1. What is a small rock called?
a) a pebble
b) a mountain
c) a boulder

2. What can you find at the centre of the Earth?
a) volcanoes
b) the core
c) treacle

3. Which of these rocks can you find on the roof of a house?
a) sandstone
b) slate
c) pumice

4. What is chalk made from?
a) metal
b) sand
c) shells

5. Which of these is a gemstone?
a) opal
b) coal
c) copper

6. What is fossilised dinosaur poo called?
a) an ore
b) a trackway
c) a trace fossil

Chalk

Gold

Gneiss

GLOSSARY

algae simple water plants, such as seaweed

ammonite an extinct mollusc that was related to squid

amphibian a cold-blooded animal, such as a frog, that breathes underwater as young and air as an adult

ancient very old

belemnite an extinct mollusc that looks similar to squid

calcite a mineral that forms limestone rock

cartilage a strong and flexible body tissue

cement lime, clay and water mixed together, which hardens and glues things together when it is dry

concrete a building material made from cement mixed with stones

crystal a natural and usually small material that forms shapes, such as triangles

dissolve when a solid breaks up in liquid

erosion the movement of material by wind or water

extinct a type of animal or plant that has died out

furnace a very large, hot oven

hatch to come out of an egg

magma a mixture of rock in that is semi-molten and forms lava after an eruption

mammal a warm-blooded animal with a skeleton and hair or fur. The young feed on their mothers' milk

microscope a scientific instrument that makes very small objects look bigger

mineral a natural material that has not come from an animal or a plant

natural something that occurs in nature and is not made by people

reptile an animal that breathes air and has dry skin covered in scales

rot break down

scallop a sea animal, related to snails, with a fan-shaped shell

stalactite an icicle-shaped piece of calcite that hangs from the roof of a cave

stalagmite a column of calcite that grows up from the floor of a cave

swamp a low area of boggy land where water collects

trilobite an extinct sea animal that looked a little like a large woodlouse

weathering materials being worn away over a long time by wind and rain

CURIOUS FACTS

CURIOUS BEGINNINGS

People have collected objects for thousands of years. During the 1500s and 1600s, special cabinets were made to display the objects that were brought back from voyages to newly-discovered lands, such as North America. These cabinets were sometimes whole rooms, which became the first museums.

WHAT IS A CURIOSITY BOX?

A curiosity box is a small copy of these cabinets. It is a more scientific way of displaying items than a nature table. You can group items together by theme. Children readily collect attractive stones and pebbles and these can form the foundation of a curiosity box all about rocks.

YOUR CURIOSITY BOX

It's easy to make your own curiosity box. A shoebox or other small cardboard box will do! Ask an adult to help you cut long strips of card with slits cut into them. Slot them together to make lots of small sections inside your box. Place the objects you find (or photographs of them) inside the sections.

It is not legal in some areas to take stones or fossils from public places. You could ask gardeners to 'donate' a stone or two from gravel. Chert, an orange brown chipping used in some gravel, may be a good starting point. Flint, limestone and sandstone chippings could also be added. Trips into your local town may reveal that prestigious buildings, such as libraries and banks, have polished granite steps and walls that could be photographed. Marble statues could also be photographed. To start a fossil collection, use the Internet to locate fossil-bearing rocks in your area, where permission for the public to collect has been granted. Some of the best places to look for small fossils are on beaches that are not in protected areas.

USEFUL INFORMATION AND WEBLINKS

Comprehensive collections of activities relating to rocks and fossils can be found at:
www.sciencekids.co.nz/geology.html
www.onegeology.org/extra/kids/what_is.html

A simple timeline of geological periods can be found at: www.funkidslive.com/earth/

ROCKS AND FOSSILS NOTES

Here is some more information, for parents and teachers, on the rocks and fossils found in this book.

What are rocks and fossils?

Looking closely in your local area can reveal different kinds of rock and, very occasionally, fossils. Many museums have fossil collections. Specimens tend to be set out according to the groups to which they belong.

Everything on Earth was once formed in the stars. Stars manufacture all of the elements that make up our universe, such as carbon and oxygen. Some elements combine to create rock-forming minerals. For example, feldspar contains elements that include aluminium, silicon and oxygen.

Earth – a rocky planet

Soil is a mixture of rocky material and humus, which is made from the bodies of dead plants and some dead animals. Bedrock may be formed of granite, limestone, sandstone or other types of rock. The crust is made up from many layers of rock.

Nobody has been (or ever could go) inside Earth to examine its structure. Information about the interior has been built up using data collected by scientists of the vibrations caused during earthquakes.

Volcanic rocks

Inside a volcano, magma contains minerals that can combine in different ways to make different kinds of rock as they cool down. Rocks that form from a volcanic eruption are called **igneous rocks**. These rocks cool down quickly and most form tiny crystals.

Rocks that form from magma trapped in the crust are also called igneous rocks. These rocks cool down slowly in the crust, which means they produce larger crystals than rocks that cooled down on the surface.

Baked rock is called **metamorphic rock**. This means a rock that changes its form. Baking occurs not only because of the heat of the magma, it can also be generated when rocks are squashed together, such as when tectonic plates push against each other.

Breaking up

During the weathering process, water inside cracks in rocks freezes, expands and pushes the rocks apart. Wind carrying sand can rub down a rock surface, and heat and cold cause expansion and contraction of rocks. This weakens it and makes it liable to break up. (Note that the term 'erosion' refers to the *transportation* of the rocky fragments.)

After the fragments have been transported away, they settle down and form sediment. Over time the sediment thickens and hardens and forms **sedimentary rocks**. Red sandstone tends to form from windblown desert sand, while other types form after travelling in water.

Rocks made from other things

Rocks made from fossilised shells are also sedimentary rocks. The most common types of fossils that make limestone are bivalve molluscs, such as clams and crinoids. (Crinoids are animals related to starfish.)

Children often mistake manufactured rocks (such as concrete) for natural rocks. The purpose of page 15 is to help children recognise these man-made items, so as not to include them in their curiosity box.

Caves and mines

Caves can form in many types of rock, such as sandstone. Stalactites and stalagmites are found in limestone caves. Limestone is made from calcium carbonate. It can be dissolved by rain, which is slightly acidic. Where drips and splashes occur, chemical reactions take place and the calcium carbonate slowly builds up to form stalactites and stalagmites.

A vein is formed from trapped magma. Different types of minerals, such as metals or gemstones, form as the vein rock cools.

Only a few metals, such as gold and tin, occur in their metallic state. They are called native metals. Other metals are combined with other elements to make rocky ores. For example iron is combined with oxygen in hematite. Smelting involves heating ores. This brings about a chemical reaction in which the metal is released from other elements.

Amber is used in jewellery, but it is not a mineral gemstone. It is fossil resin produced by conifers. Some amber has insects trapped inside.

Coal and sandstone fossils

Most plant fossils form by a process of carbonisation, where the body is reduced to its carbon content. This carbon can become coal, which is a useful fuel. Most animal fossils form as shown on page 21. The other type of animal fossil forms when minerals seep into the tissues of the body and strengthen them to make the whole body turn to stone.

Ammonites and belemnites are invertebrate molluscs related to the octopus and squid. The fossils featured on these pages are common ones that may be found in areas known for their fossil-bearing rocks. The devil's claw is a type of oyster. A brachiopod has two shells like a clam, but they open in a different way.

More animal fossils

Shark teeth are made of calcium, which forms fossils easily, whereas their cartilage skeletons do not. All vertebrates with skeletons of bone can form fossils. By studying the fossils of living things, it has been possible to see how certain kinds of animal have changed over long periods of time. For example, today's birds are related to feathered dinosaurs. Information has been used to construct a theory of evolution.

Trace fossils

Trace fossils were generally made by a body as it moved. For example fossil burrows, called *Thalassinoides*, were typically made by a type of shrimp. Footprints are the most famous trace fossils. A series of footprints is called a trackway and have been produced by: reptile-like animals before the age of the dinosaurs; the dinosaurs themselves; and animals, such as the Moa (a large ostrich-like bird), which came after the dinosaurs. Dinosaurs are not the only animals to leave fossilised droppings. Mammoths from the Ice Age have left them, too.